Let's Visit the Library

Marianne Johnston

The Rosen Publishing Group's
PowerKids Press™
New York

CCC

Published in 2000 by The Rosen Publishing Group, Inc.
29 East 21st Street, New York, NY 10010

First Edition

Book design: Danielle Primiceri

Photo Credits and Illustrations: Cover, pp. 4, 8, 11, 12, 15, 19, 20 by Bonnie Rothstein-Brewer; p. 7 © CORBIS/Bettmann; p. 9 © Victoria & Albert Museum/Art Resource; p. 16 © Stan Riestea/International Stock; p. 17 © Barry Rosenthal/FPG International.

Johnston, Marianne.
        Let's visit the library / by Marianne Johnston.
                p.   cm. — (Our community)
        Includes index.
        Summary: Describes libraries, the functions that they perform, and the role these institutions play in the community.
        ISBN 0-8239-5431-5 (lib. bdg. : alk. paper)
        1. Public libraries Juvenile literature [1. Libraries] I. Title. II. Series: Johnston, Marianne.
        Our community.
        Z665.5.J64   1999
        027.4—dc21   99-19101
                                                                                     CIP

Manufactured in the United States of America

Contents

The Library

Are you interested in dinosaurs or ballet? Would you like to watch a videotape about your favorite baseball player or listen to music from Africa? If your answer is yes, then it's time to head for your library!

The library serves the **community** by storing and lending out lots of books. The library is also a special place where you can learn new things about the world and about your community.

You never know who you'll run into at the library.

5

Where Did Libraries Begin?

About 5,000 years ago, the people of Egypt and Babylonia stored **collections** of religious writings in their temples. They also kept government records in their royal palaces. As time passed, teachers and religious leaders added to the collections. More and more people visited to read these writings. As the collections got bigger and more people used them, they became known as libraries.

FUN FACTS

One of the most famous libraries of the past was the Library of Alexandria in Egypt.

Ancient libraries were mostly used by scholars and religious people.

Modern Libraries

Today, almost every community has a library. In the past, cities or counties had one large library. Starting about 100 years ago, people thought it was important to put smaller libraries in many different neighborhoods so people wouldn't have to travel a long way to get to one. In the 1930s, a group of people in Kentucky even ran a library on horseback to make sure everyone could get the books they wanted to read.

FUN FACTS

In 1456, Johan Gutenberg printed the first book using movable type.

Today there are many libraries because most people can read and books are easy to produce.

The Dewey Decimal System

Libraries would be very hard to use if they didn't have a way to organize their books. To do this, all libraries use something called the **Dewey Decimal System**. In this system, each book in the library gets a **call number** that shows where it belongs on the shelf. Books get numbered according to subject. If the book is about science, then the call number is between 600 and 699. If it is about religion, then the call number is between 200 and 299, and so on. The call numbers appear on the spine of the book and are the same no matter what library you use.

With the Dewey Decimal system, each subject gets its own group of numbers. ▶

People at the Library

Different people at the library have different jobs. Desk assistants can help you find a particular book, or just check out the ones you've chosen. You can usually find them at the front desk of the library.

The reference librarians often have their own desks. Their job is to help you find information. If you have a school project, they're the ones to talk to.

Pages move around the library putting books back on the shelf in the right order. This way, the next person who wants to read a book can find the one she's looking for.

◄ *People who work at the library can help you find the book you're looking for.*

Volunteers

It takes a lot of work to run a library. Most libraries need **volunteers** from the community to help out. Volunteers help the community by working for free.

When Laura goes to the library, the first person she sees is her next door neighbor, Mrs. Taylor. Mrs. Taylor volunteers to help the desk assistants check out books. In the reading room, Laura sees her baby-sitter reading to kids for story hour. Maybe you could help out at your library by reading to kids who are younger than you, or by putting books away.

Volunteers do not get paid for their work at the library. ▸

The Library of Congress

The Library of Congress is the biggest library in the United States. It was founded in 1800 by the U.S. government. It has more than 17 million books, which fill 532 miles of shelves! Since the Library of Congress is America's national library, the library staff works to collect many books, maps, films, and photographs by Americans or on American history. It is a library for the entire American community.

FUN FACTS

More than two million people visit the Library of Congress each year.

Nearly 5,000 people work for the Library of Congress.

Computers and the Library

In the past, if you wanted to find a book at your community library, you had to use the **card catalog**. Now, in most libraries, all that information is also stored in the **on-line catalog**. To find a book, all you have to do is go to the library computer and type in the title, author, or subject. Some libraries also have Web sites that you can use to see what books the library has without even leaving your home.

FUN FACTS

Some libraries have computers people can use to get on-line and onto the World Wide Web.

http://www.loc.gov

Computers have made it easier to use the library. ▶

How the Library Works

Barbara needed a book about dogs. She asked the reference librarian for help. The librarian typed the word "dog" into the on-line catalog and the call numbers of several books came up. Barbara used the call numbers to find where the books on dogs were located. Once she found her book, Barbara went to the front desk to check it out. The desk assistant placed a **due date** card in the book. If Barbara returned the book to the library after the due date, she would have to pay a **fine**.

◀ *It's important to return books by their due dates.*

Libraries Are Community Centers

The people in your community can get a lot out of a library besides books. It is a great place to go to get information for school projects. Libraries usually have a special section where kids can go to read. Be sure to check out your library and all it has to offer you. Maybe you'll even volunteer and find out that you have something to offer your library!

Web Sites:

For more information on the Library of Congress, check out this Web site: http://www.loc.gov

Glossary

call number (KAHL NUHM-ber) The number on a book that shows where on the library shelf that book belongs.

card catalog (KARD KAT-uh-log) An alphabetical list of library items that is stored on separate cards and kept in a cabinet.

collection (cuh-LEK-shun) A group of similar objects, like books, that are collected over time.

community (kuh-MYOO-nih-tee) A group of people who have something in common, such as a special interest or the area where they live.

Dewey Decimal System (DOO-wee DEH-sih-mul SIS-tum) The system community libraries use to organize their book collections.

due date (DOO DAYT) The day that you must return the items that you borrowed from the library.

fine (FYN) A small payment you must make to the library if you turn your borrowed items in after their due dates.

on-line catalog (ON-LYN KAT-uh-log) A system of storing information about library books on computers.

volunteers (vah-lun-TEERZ) People who work for free.

Index